BLAH TO
Fierce

FOR WOMEN WHO ARE STUCK IN A RUT

SHEKINA FARR MOORE
GIRLS ADVOCATE &
FEMALE EMPOWERMENT TRAINER

Shekina Moore
GIRLS ADVOCATE

LITERACY MOGULS™

DEDICATION

To the young woman with the tough exterior,
who cries herself to sleep at night—You have
the goods.

CONTENTS

ACKNOWLEDGMENTS

To my husband who is always in my corner
and births with me.
To my sister Tonia who has supported me from
day one in more ways than I can count.
To my mother who is a constant encourager.
To my father for being ever present and setting
a standard.
To Deanna & Barbara who showed me what
tenacity looked like in the right season. You
fierce divas encourage me.
To my baby boys Colin and Lance who allowed
mommy to complete this book so that women
may be touched around the world.
To Oprah who is my mentor from afar.

INTRODUCTION

You may be asking yourself, is this a book I need? Am I *blah*?

Blah is described as insipid; dull; uninteresting; a feeling of physical uneasiness, general discomfort, or mild depression.
It may be difficult to admit you are *blah*. So, the real question is, "Are you *fierce?*"
Urban Dictionary describes *fierce* as being bold, displaying chutzpah; absolutely everything of "exceptional quality."
Even if you find you are somewhere in the middle, skirting by, this book is for *you*.
Interestingly, the conception of this book began with a simple conversation I was having with a friend who was in a great season of her life, exemplifying *exceptional quality*, while I was on the polar opposite end of the spectrum. She was looking good, smelling good, talking good and exuding good. Meanwhile, I had just moved and was in an uncomfortable place in my life. I had a baby, gained 77 lbs and moved to another city. I was stressed. So, while I was happy for my friend, I was also nostalgic. What happened to *me*? I was that spunky go-getter with the cute *bod* and consecutive great hair days. Now, I'm this frumpy chic with no *je ne sais quoi?*
It was at that moment that I decided to challenge myself to get back to me! I took inventory and, with some work, I made it

happen! The result is on the cover of this book. *Me ...reinvented.*

Each day, for 30 days, I did something that compounded and excited me. Excitement is a great thing! I believe it to be the key ingredient in my success. People are attracted and drawn to people with excitement and energy. My hope now is for women who are in a rut, like I found myself, to take this challenge and get their *mojo* back. If you are reading this book, IT IS YOUR TIME!

Seizing your time only requires mind renewal. There is a story I love that helps me to envision mind renewal and so I will share it with you.

Imagine that you have lived in your home for 20 years of your life.

You've memorized the fastest ways to drive back from your work, from church, from your friend's place, from school, and from the gym. You've developed a route that you take every time. *You don't think about it,* that's just the way you go home because you've done that for 20 years. You know the correct turns to make. You know the best time to take which route based on how bad traffic is. You know which roads have the most cops. And you know all the ins and outs of getting yourself home.

Then imagine if you move 10 minutes away.

The next day, you are about to head back home from work. You get in your car as usual, and you start driving. Out of sheer habit and muscle memory, you take the same old highway, the same old exit, and the same traffic all the way until you get home, only to realize that *you no longer live at your old house.* You slap yourself on the forehead thinking, "How could I forget?! I moved! Gotta make sure I don't do this again…what a waste of time!"

The next day is similar, you get into your car and you begin to take the same route you've taken for the last 20 years. It isn't until about halfway home you realize again, "Shoot! I moved!" You pull a U-turn and head towards the new home you recently moved into.

So by this point, you're consciously making an effort to make sure it doesn't happen again. You create a reminder in your head, "Alright, when I reach this street, I have to make a left where I used to make a right." You know it will take a conscious effort to forge a new pattern because the old pattern was so familiar, natural and comfortable. But you know you have to do it because you no longer live at the old house– none of your belongings are there. Plus, the new house is much bigger, with *a lot more freedom* to move around.

The next day, as you leave your house for work, you make another mental note to remind yourself that you've moved so that you won't forget at the end of the day. The time arrives, and you get into your car. Confident, reminding

3

yourself that you have a new home, you get all the way home without taking a wrong turn. When you arrive, you breathe a sigh of satisfaction, knowing that you took the right route and you're confident it'll be easier next time.

Over a period of a few weeks, *what started with lots of errors and mistakes starts to become second-nature and natural.* The muscle memory and old pattern of thinking was undone and *now it's hard to imagine ever taking that old route again.* In addition to that, you've done the same exercise with your church, school, friend's place, and the gym. All the old routes were reprogrammed and redesigned to fit the location of your new home.

Months down the road, it's *nowhere near a struggle.* You've forged a new routine— a new habit. You arrive at your new home every time. And every once in a while, you'll be at an intersection you used to use when you were at your old house, and you'll get a familiar feeling of when you used to slam the pedal to try to make the light...you reminisce on the memories. But then you'd snap back into reality remembering, "Well...I don't live there anymore."

"Renewing your mind" is definitely not just about reciting a list of facts. Nor is it about confessing a phrase in an effort to try to persuade yourself to believe it. When you renew your mind, it should renew the way you do things. A new perspective should result in a new set of actions, just like moving to *a new house will cause you to take new directions*. Taking new directions aren't a requirement, but it's a natural byproduct of understanding that you have a new house.

The problem is that it will still feel natural and I will be tempted to take the old route toward the old house if I believe I still live there. I will allow the habit and the muscle memory to dictate my direction if I never realize the fact that I have a new house. But if I'm truly convinced that I have moved, I will make every conscious effort to take the new route every time. Why? Because I've moved. The new house is better than the old house, and all my belongings are in the new one.

So, if you are ready to stop driving to your old house (*Blah-dom*) and you are at a place where you can receive all that is yours at *Fierce-dom,* I invite you to take this 30-day challenge to *"Speak It! Become It! Own It! & Flaunt It!"*

Just remember, this is a personal journey. Tell no one. *Shhh......*

SHEKINA FARR MOORE

"It takes courage to grow up and become who you really are."
E.E. Cummings

6

Week One: Speak It (Inner)

DAY 1: LOOK YOURSELF IN THE EYE AND PROCLAIM WHO YOU ARE

Focused affirmations are a great way to start your new tomorrows. When you feel tension, stress, or any type of anxiety, an affirmation that makes you feel good is where you need to go. My favorite is: I AM POWERFUL. It makes me feel so good! However, for the affirmations to work you must not only say something which makes you feel better, you have to FEEL the words.

So! Say whatever makes you feel good, then *see* yourself in a happy scenario doing or being your desire. See it, feel it, even taste it! The more emotion you have the faster you will draw it to you. Here are some affirmations you might use, but the best ones are ones you make up yourself:

- I AM POWERFUL
- MONEY COMES TO ME
- LOVE COMES TO ME
- GREAT HEALTH COMES TO ME
- I AM AT MY IDEAL WEIGHT
- I AM BALANCED AND CENTERED
- I AM IN PERFECT HEALTH
- I GIVE AND RECEIVE LOVE ALWAYS

- I AM JOYFUL
- I LOOK AND FEEL WONDERFUL

If it takes saying them over and over a thousand times a day, then do it. If you say an affirmation when you are feeling really down, and you don't think it's doing anything for you, just keep on. Every time you say something positive you will bit by bit feel better. A little bit of feeling better is better than lots of feeling depressed.

You only have power in the *now*. The past is gone. It cannot ever be changed and tomorrow is always uncertain. If you want to change your life, choose to start NOW, in this moment, this is the moment of your power, your choice.

Are you fed up with repeating the same old patterns from the past, continually sabotaging your future? Do you want to break out of the life you are in now to a new wonderful life where you achieve and experience the life that *you* want?

"Man often becomes what he believes himself to be. If I keep on saying to myself that I cannot do a certain thing, it is possible that I may end by really becoming incapable of doing it. On the contrary, if I have the belief that I can do it, I shall surely acquire the capacity to do it even if I may not have it at the beginning."
Mahatma Gandhi

DAY 2: DISPEL THE MYTHS YOU TOLD YOURSELF WHEN YOU WERE DOWN

When you were in the thick of it the haze was so thick you couldn't see two feet in front of you. You were consumed with your illness, your move, your divorce, your new baby, your loss, your lay-off, your audit. It was the season for you to be in the thick of it. You certainly are a woman of strength to have endured and live to tell it. But now, it is time for renewal, time to get back to *you*. So, the names you called yourself and the names you answered to can no longer have place in your life. The myths you told yourself when you were down you must now relinquish to move forward. Some of these myths are delaying your destiny and others are holding you back altogether.

Let's see if some of these myths sound familiar:

"I am so far gone."
"I am out of time; expired"
"It's been so long since I looked like that I wouldn't recognize myself if I _____"
"Nobody notices the change."
Replace these negative thoughts with the Source. What does the Source say about who you are? Did you know that with *The Source* there is a laundry list? This tells me He thinks of me and you often.
Remind yourself of this today and every day:

11

I am a child of God.

But to all who have received him--those who believe in his name--he has given the right to become God's children ... (John 1:12).

I am a branch of the true vine, and a conduit of Christ's life.

I am the true vine and my Father is the gardener. I am the vine; you are the branches. The one who remains in me--and I in him--bears much fruit, because apart from me you can accomplish nothing (John 15:1, 5).

I am a friend of Jesus.

I no longer call you slaves, because the slave does not understand what his master is doing. But I have called you friends, because I have revealed to you everything I heard from my Father (John 15:15).

I have been justified and redeemed.

But they are justified freely by his grace through the redemption that is in Christ Jesus (Romans 3:24).

My old self was crucified with Christ, and I am no longer a slave to sin.

We know that our old man was crucified with him so that the body of sin would no longer dominate us, so that we would no longer be enslaved to sin (Romans 6:6).

I will not be condemned by God.

There is therefore now no condemnation for those who are in Christ Jesus (Romans 8:1).

I have been set free from the law of sin and death.

For the law of the life-giving Spirit in Christ Jesus has set you free from the law of sin and death (Romans 8:2).

As a child of God, I am a fellow heir with Christ.

And if children, then heirs (namely, heirs of God and also fellow heirs with Christ)--if indeed we suffer with him so we may also be glorified with him (Romans 8:17).

I have been accepted by Christ.

Receive one another, then, just as Christ also received you, to God's glory (Romans 15:7).

I have been called to be a saint.

… To the church of God that is in Corinth, to those who are sanctified in Christ Jesus, and called to be saints, with all those in every place

who call on the name of our Lord Jesus Christ, their Lord and ours (1 Corinthians 1:2). (See also Ephesians 1:1, Philippians 1:1, and Colossians 1:2.)

In Christ Jesus, I have wisdom, righteousness, sanctification, and redemption.

He is the reason you have a relationship with Christ Jesus, who became for us wisdom from God, and righteousness and sanctification and redemption ... (1 Corinthians 1:30).

My body is a temple of the Holy Spirit who dwells in me.

Do you not know that you are God's temple and that God's Spirit lives in you (1 Corinthians 6:19)?

I am joined to the Lord and am one spirit with Him.

But the one united with the Lord is one spirit with him (1 Corinthians 6:17).

God leads me in the triumph and knowledge of Christ.

But thanks be to God who always leads us in triumphal procession in Christ and who makes known through us the fragrance that consists of the knowledge of him in every place (2

Corinthians 2:14).

The hardening of my mind has been removed in Christ.

But their minds were closed. For to this very day, the same veil remains when they hear the old covenant has not been removed because only in Christ is it taken away (2 Corinthians 3:14).

I am a new creature in Christ.

So then, if anyone is in Christ, he is a new creation; what is old has passed away--look, what is new has come (2 Corinthians 5:17)!

I have become the righteousness of God in Christ.

God made the one who did not know sin to be sin for us, so that in him we would become the righteousness of God (2 Corinthians 5:21).

I have been made one with all who are in Christ Jesus.

There is neither Jew nor Greek, there is neither slave nor free, there is neither male nor female--for all of you are one in Christ Jesus (Galatians 3:28).

I am no longer a slave, but a child and an heir.

So you are no longer a slave but a son, and if you are a son, then you are also an heir through God (Galatians 4:7).

I have been set free in Christ.

For freedom Christ has set us free. Stand firm, then, and do not be subject again to the yoke of slavery (Galatians 5:1).

I have been blessed with every spiritual blessing in the heavenly places.

Blessed is the God and Father of our Lord Jesus Christ, who has blessed us with every spiritual blessing in the heavenly realms in Christ (Ephesians 1:3).

I am chosen, holy, and blameless before God.

For he chose us in Christ before the foundation of the world that we may be holy and unblemished in his sight in love (Ephesians 1:4).

I am redeemed and forgiven by the grace of Christ.

In him we have redemption through his blood, the forgiveness of our trespasses, according to the riches of his grace (Ephesians 1:7).

I have been predestined by God to obtain an

inheritance.

In Christ we too have been claimed as God's own possession, since we were predestined according to the one purpose of him who accomplishes all things according to the counsel of his will (Ephesians 1:11).

I have been sealed with the Holy Spirit of promise.

And when you heard the word of truth (the gospel of your salvation)--when you believed in Christ--you were marked with the seal of the promised Holy Spirit (Ephesians 1:13).

Because of God's mercy and love, I have been made alive with Christ.

But God, being rich in mercy, because of his great love with which he loved us, even though we were dead in transgressions, made us alive together with Christ--by grace you are saved (Ephesians 2:4-5)!

I am seated in the heavenly places with Christ.

… And he raised us up with him and seated us with him in the heavenly realms in Christ Jesus … (Ephesians 2:6).

I am God's workmanship created to produce good works.

For we are his workmanship, having been created in Christ Jesus for good works that God prepared beforehand so we may do them (Ephesians 2:10).

I have been brought near to God by the blood of Christ.

But now in Christ Jesus you who used to be far away have been brought near by the blood of Christ (Ephesians 2:13).

I am a member of Christ's body and a partaker of His promise.

... The Gentiles are fellow heirs, fellow members of the body, and fellow partakers of the promise in Christ Jesus (Ephesians 3:6). (See also Ephesians 5:30.)

I have boldness and confident access to God through faith in Christ.

... In whom we have boldness and confident access to God because of Christ's faithfulness (Ephesians 3:12).

My new self is righteous and holy.

... Put on the new man who has been created in God's image--in righteousness and holiness that comes from truth (Ephesians 4:24). I was formerly darkness, but now I am light in the Lord.

18

… For you were at one time darkness, but now you are light in the Lord. Walk as children of the light (Ephesians 5:8).

I am a citizen of heaven.

But our citizenship is in heaven--and we also await a savior from there, the Lord Jesus Christ … (Philippians 3:20).

The peace of God guards my heart and mind.

And the peace of God that surpasses all understanding will guard your hearts and minds in Christ Jesus (Philippians 4:7).

God supplies all my needs.

And my God will supply your every need according to his glorious riches in Christ Jesus (Philippians 4:19).

I have been made complete in Christ.

… You have been filled in him, who is the head over every ruler and authority (Colossians 2:10).

I have been raised up with Christ.

Therefore, if you have been raised with Christ, keep seeking the things above, where Christ is, seated at the right hand of God (Colossians

3:1).

My life is hidden with Christ in God.

… For you have died and your life is hidden with Christ in God (Colossians 3:3).

Christ is my life, and I will be revealed with Him in glory.

When Christ (who is your life) appears, then you too will be revealed in glory with him (Colossians 3:4).

I have been chosen of God, and I am holy and beloved.

Therefore, as the elect of God, holy and dearly loved, clothe yourselves with a heart of mercy, kindness, humility, gentleness, and patience … (Colossians 3:12).

God loves me and has chosen me.

We know, brothers and sisters loved by God, that he has chosen you …
(1 Thessalonians 1:4).

Why?

The more we embrace these truths from Scripture about who we have become in Christ, the more stable, grateful, and fully assured we will be in this world.

You see, clearly God sees us differently than we often see ourselves. The question is whose report do you believe?

This brings me a poignant point about our judgment. It is at best limited. This may be the rationale behind the *What Would Jesus Do* phenomenon that rocked the nation some time ago. The phrase "*What would Jesus do?*" (often abbreviated to WWJD) became popular in the United States in the 1990s and as a personal motto for adherents of Evangelical Christianity who used the phrase as a reminder of their belief in a moral imperative to act in a manner that would demonstrate the love of Jesus through the actions of the adherents. Many bracelets displaying WWJD were worn as a reminder of the principle.

So, in moving away from your *blah* state to one that connects you with your audience in a relevant and authentic way, I pose to you a burning question, one for *you* to ask *yourself* over the course of this challenge…

21

DAY 3: ASK YOURSELF
WHAT WOULD FIERCE AMY DO?

Amy knew she had a passion for restaurant administration and wanted to own her own restaurant one day but she always felt she was not good enough. She didn't feel she looked the part and she certainly didn't feel anyone would give her the keys to a business.

The single most driving factor behind all of our fears in life has to do with us feeling inadequate.

Despite feelings of inadequacy Amy decided to attend a National Convention her boss had recommended while she was working as a restaurant manager. She had no intentions of the conference changing her life but she did understand that important people in her industry would be speaking and it would certainly be an opportunity for her to learn.

It is okay to be afraid, it is not okay to allow being afraid to stop you from moving.

In groups, Amy brought out some great points on ways to improve customer retention. All at the table were in awe. Amy knew her craft and was comfortable expressing herself in the intimate group. However, when the group insisted Amy speak at the podium to share insights on behalf of the group, fear overcame her like never before.

Amy was at a crossroads.

Maybe you are scared to present an idea to a group because you feel you're not experienced enough.

Or maybe you can't fully love someone else because inside you feel like you can't love *yourself* unconditionally.

Or maybe you just want to start a new hobby that you think you'll enjoy, but you never do because you hate being the newbie.

I'm right there with you. I hate feeling inexperienced. I hate learning something new in front of others. I hate not knowing.

But it's all a part of life. There's no way any of us can be experts in everything, have full confidence in every situation, and jump into something new like we've done it 20 times before.

There's just too much in this world to be that good.

"Not knowing is growing"– Accepting that we're inadequate and don't know everything is the first step. But beyond that, we need to put a positive, proactive spin to it. About 10 years ago Amy was given the task to stand up in front

23

of about 500 peers and executives at a restauranteur's conference to talk about something. She didn't want to. She never said "no" or anything like that, but deep inside she knew she would rather curl up in a ball somewhere instead.

After her speech she had people coming up to her telling her (and her boss at the time) how well she delivered the message. It was total growth. From then on, Amy wasn't 100% comfortable with that group but it took an enormous weight off her shoulders. When you jump into the unknown it's a guarantee that you will come out at the other end knowing more.

Look at your idols/role-models– I think we all have certain people in our lives that we look up to and want to be like. We put this sort of halo around them that they are perfect and if we could be like them then all would be well. When you feel inadequate look at them *for them*, not your perception. Look into their past failures and how they overcame them.

EX.
Amy runs a multimillion dollar business and has built a family restaurant empire and she looks fabulous. She overcame a 100 lbs weight-gain after her last son was born and her first restaurant was demolished in a natural disaster.

Journal, journal, and journal– One thing that has been extremely helpful for me in the past couple of years is *journaling*. Take a moment right now to write down something that you've recently accomplished that you're proud of. Write down some things you hope to accomplish and remember to date your entry.

Try to journal at least once a week with this same information. This practice helps with the now but even more so in the future when you can look back and remember all of the things you've done and maybe even some of the things you accomplished that you wanted to. As you go on in life, it's easy to be too humble about some of the things you've done and you forget all about them. Journaling doesn't allow you to forget.

Small decisions to keep moving in a positive direction toward her dreams and aspirations helps Amy to be FIERCE! After Amy courageously stepped to that podium as a manager in front of 500+ top executives, she began to change. Whenever she was faced with fear, she simply began to ask herself, what would Fierce Amy do? Fierce Amy did things a little differently than *Blah Amy*. *Blah Amy* would second-guess herself a lot, eat poorly, self-sabotage, take no risks, apologize for wanting more in life and put herself last. Fierce Amy was decisive, planned her life, took chances, researched business plans, upgraded her associations and dressed like a boss. Amy began to grow!

Had Amy allowed fear to stop her from making the types of small decisions that propelled her career into overdrive, Amy would likely still be living a *blah* life with a *blah* boyfriend, in a *blah* town wearing *blah* clothes, holding *blah* conversations about *blah* events.

So, the next time you are tempted to by a *blah* existence, ask yourself what would *Fierce Amy* do?

DAY 4: TAKE INVENTORY OF YOUR PEEPS

Negativity can be, and far too often is, contagious! Just like a virus, it goes from person to person, wreaking havoc on all with weak immune systems. Be mindful of this vice as it can have a more far-reaching influence on your life than most of us are aware of. Do what you can to surround yourself with positive, upbeat, helpful, and hopeful people.

Co-workers
This one sneaks up on you. Most of our social groups form at work and in business. As an educator I recall everyone around me drinking coffee. Before long, I was a coffee drinker. Imagine all the habits that you have picked up just by being apart of your work environment. Who are some of the negative influencers? Jot them down.

_____
_____
_____
_____
_____

Family
This one is tricky. After all, you can't help what family you were born into, right? Right. But you can help who you spend exhaustive amounts of time with and the topics you entertain. Who in your family makes you cringe when you see

them coming because they are so negative?
Jot this down.

_____

_____

_____

_____

_____

Friends
I saved the best for last. You know I did. This
can be a sensitive topic because these are
individuals you choose to hang around. But a
lot of the time, you still go out of your way to
salvage messy relationships for a variety of
reasons: you've known the individual for a long
time; they've *got issues*; they have good
intentions, and so on and so forth. These are
people that you know you have outgrown yet
you continue to spend time with them as they
zap you of energy.

Here are some tell-tale signs you have
outgrown your circle:

-You only converse through emails, texts &
social media.
-When you talk, your conversation lacks depth.
-You have grown closer with other people with
similar interests.
-When you need them they are nowhere to be
found.
-They now participate in activities you once
said you would never do.

28

-You want to talk ideas, dreams and aspirations; they want to talk about people and things.

Some co-workers, colleagues, family and friends cannot be cajoled, badgered, counseled, or even beaten out of a negative attitude about life and everything in it! If you have many friends like this, be aware of how this affects your mood. Take inventory. If you find, as many do, that this negativity has a wearing effect on your attitude, you may want to consider the company you keep. After all, birds of a feather flock together.

"Ninety-nine percent of the failures come from people who have the habit of making excuses."
George Washington Carver

DAY 5: WRITE YOUR EXCUSE LIST

You've convinced yourself that there is no escaping; that the situation you are in must be permanent. Or you are on the opposite end and you know there is a way out but you have a million reasons why today is not the day to get unstuck.

WAKE UP! SNAP OUT OF IT! It is not about you. You have a flock of people waiting on you. They need what you have and no one else can give them what they need like you can.
There is an exhaustive list of "reasons" you are choosing to stay in your predicament. However, most excuses boil down to this one excuse:

Time
You think too much time has elapsed. You think your ship has sailed. You think you missed your season. You think you body won't snap back because you let it go so far off course. You think your sex appeal eludes you. You think your age gives you an out. You really think your *carpe diem* opportunity is gone. Well, beautiful, I have news for you. Not only are you at the right time of your life with the right book in your hand, you belong to a RIGHT God who holds all time in His hands. The excuses you cling to shall no longer hold you captive from what He already said is YOURS. J.K.Rowling was 30 years old when she

31

finished the first manuscript for Harry Potter.

Amelia Earhart was 31 years old when she became the first woman to fly solo across the Atlantic Ocean.

Oprah was 32 when she started her talk show, which became the highest-rated program of its kind.

Edmund Hillary was 33 when he became the first man to reach Mount Everest (highest Mountain in the world.

Martin Luther King Jr. was 34 When he did the speech "I have a dream".

Marie Curie was 35 years old when she got nominated for the Nobel Prize in Physics 1903.

The Wright brothers, (Orville was 32 & Wilbur was 36) when they invented & built the world's first successful airplane & made the first controlled, powered & sustained heavier-than-air human flight.
Vincent Van Gogh was 37 when he died virtually unknown, yet his paintings today are worth millions.

Neil Armstrong was 38 when he became the first man to set foot on the moon.

Mark Twain was 40 when he wrote The

Adventures of Tom Sawyer and 49 years old when he wrote Adventures of Huckleberry Finn.

Christopher Columbus was 41 when he discovered the Americas.

Rosa Parks was 42 when she refused to obey the bus driver's order to give up her seat to make room for a white passenger.

John F. Kennedy was 43 years old when he became President of the United States.

Henry Ford Was 45 when the *Ford T* came out.

Suzanne Collins was 46 when she wrote *The Hunger Games.*

Charles Darwin was 50 years old when his book On the *Origin of Species* came out.

Leonardo Da Vinci was 51 years old when he painted the Mona Lisa.

Abraham Lincoln was 52 when he became President.

Ray Kroc Was 53 when he bought the McDonald's franchise and took it to unprecedented levels.

Dr. Seuss was 54 when he wrote The Cat in the Hat.

Chesley "Sully" Sullenberger III was 57 years old when he successfully ditched US Airways Flight1549 in the Hudson River in 2009. All of the 155 passengers aboard the aircraft survived.

Colonel Harland Sanders was 61 when he started the KFC franchise.

J R R Tolkien was 62 when the Lord of the Rings books came out.

Ronald Reagan was 69 when he became President of the United States.

Jack Lalane at age 70 handcuffed, shackled and towed 70 rowboats.

Nelson Mandela was 76 when he became President.

You see, you are never too old to live victoriously. I imagine these individuals kept their eye gates, ear gates and visions protected as they pursued their passions with no apology.

"YOU ARE THE SAME TODAY THAT YOU ARE GOING TO BE IN FIVE YEARS FROM NOW EXCEPT FOR TWO THINGS: THE PEOPLE WITH WHOM YOU ASSOCIATE AND THE BOOKS YOU READ."
CHARLES JONES

DAY 6: READ TO RENEW YOUR MIND

Before getting specific, let's just begin with the most rudimentary basics of reading. Reading has ripple-effect benefits that manifest in layers with variance.
I have found that no matter what I read, the act of reading every day has helped me in nearly every aspect of my life. Here are a few of my favorite ways that reading has improved my quality of life, and will definitely improve yours.

I have improved memory. Reading on a consistent basis literally helps me with retention and recall.

I have smarts. Women who read have higher intelligence and sharper minds as they age.

I have reduced stress. When I am engaged in a great book, my mind is in heaven.

I have clarity of thought. Reading puts me in a place of tranquility where I can be still long enough to get clear and focused.

I enjoy increased vocabulary. At times others think I am "showing off" when, in fact, I am doing what comes natural.

It's no secret that reading increases your vocabulary and improves your spelling, but did you know that reading increases your vocabulary more than talking or direct teaching? Reading forces us to look at words that we might not have otherwise seen or heard.

Increased vocabulary is especially crucial for writers. In order to write well, you need to read. A beefier vocabulary is also great for knowing what other people are saying and using the perfect words to convey your own feelings. The ability to pull from an arsenal of vocabulary is empowering.

Reading has also helped me to zero in on patterns quickly.

Best of all, reading makes me a great listener, which makes me a better person.

Now, let's talk about what you are reading.

Whatever it is, make sure it is building you, speaking to where you are destined, equipping you with a can-do mindset and edifying the powerhouse of a woman you are.

There are a plethora of books that do just that. I thought I would share some of my choices:

- The 10 Laws of Enduring Success, by Maria Bartiromo
- Knowing Your Value, by Mika Brzezinski
- Your Million Dollar Dream, by Tamara Monosoff

- The E-Myth, by Michael E. Gerber
- Creating Money, by Sanaya Roman & Duane Packer
- Women Don't Ask, by Linda Babcock
- The Go-Getter Girl's Guide, by Debra Shigley
- How Remarkable Women Lead, by Joanna Barsh and Susie Cranston
- Brag! The Art of Tooting Your Own Horn Without Blowing It, by Peggy Klaus
- The Next Generation of Women Leaders: What You Need to Lead but Won't Learn in Business School, by Selena Rezvani
- Nice Girls Don't Get the Corner Office, by Lois Frankel, PhD
- Getting from College to Career, by Lindsey Pollak
- Basic Black: The Essential Guide for Getting Ahead at Work (and in Life), by Cathie Black
- Ask For It: How Women Can Use the Power of Negotiation to Get What They Really Want, by Linda Babcock and Sara Laschever
- The Best Advice I Ever Got: Lessons from Extraordinary Lives, by Katie Couric
- Lean In, by Sheryl Sandberg

- She Wins, You Win: The Most Important Rule Every Businesswoman Needs to Know, by Gail Evans

There has to be more than a cute face, lips, hips and finger tips. If you are serious about being *fierce*, get knowledge.

It is by no coincidence that this book is in your hands. Take Day 6 challenge by the reigns and stop by your local bookstore and pick up a few of the books to begin reading. This list will not disappoint you and each will help to propel you!

DAY 7: SCHEDULE *YOU* APPOINTMENTS

Now, say it with me, "I have neglected myself too long. I take care of others best when I've taken care of me first." Let it penetrate. Say it again, "I have neglected myself too long. I take care of others best when I've taken care of me first."

Now, pick up the phone and schedule out all of the following appointments for the year. DO IT TODAY.

–manicure/pedicure

–hair

–massage

–dental cleaning

–eyebrow shaping

–gynecologist

–optometrist

–nutritionist

These appointments are not options. Your hair, nails and brows must be groomed. Your teeth must be cleaned and whitened. Your health must be priority. Your eyes must be checked.

They are requirements. If you are not taken care of, how dare you attempt to take care of another? How long will you hold up doing so? What tends to happen is you burn out and you are no good for anyone or anything by then. Instead, take care of you like no one else can. This is a part of loving yourself, caring for yourself, keeping your temple acceptable unto God.

Next, get clear about your budget. This way you can get clear about the frequency of your routine appointments. Ideally, you should aim to frequent the hair salon and nail spa twice a month. Your brows should be groomed at least twice a week. You should get a massage at least bi-monthly. Your doctors may best assist you with your respective exam schedules.

Stay on top of this starting today so that you can shine bright like a diamond!

Week Two:
Become It
(Hygiene &
Maintenance)

DAY 8: REVAMP YOUR PANTY DRAWER

That's right. Get it tight. Your panty drawer is a tell-tale sign of your sex life. Believe it or not when you have the confidence that your lingerie is on point, it boosts your libido. This provides vitality and youthful energy that undoubtedly makes you feel *desirable*!

Here are 10 lingerie essentials every woman needs in her lingerie drawer. These are the basics that will give you a good foundation for every piece in your closet, whether it's the heat of summer, the dead of winter, a fancy evening out, or a relaxed afternoon in. They are trend-proof, flexible, and absolute time savers.

Bras

T-shirt Bra–As the name suggests, t-shirt bras are perfect for wearing under anything tight, close-fitting, or thin. Because the bra is constructed of one, seamless piece, you won't end up with those annoying boob-shaped lines under your clothes. In addition, the molded cups make them great for evening and shaping the breasts without adding padding or bulk.

Nude Bra--When you want to wear light or white-colored clothing, a nude bra is a wardrobe essential. Many people equate nude with one beige or tan shade, but, in reality, nude is whatever matches your skin tone.

43

MySkins is the only company manufacturing nude bras in 20 different shades, and while it's not perfect, it is the best thing out there at the moment and a great option for most women.

Convertible Bra—Because not all your clothing has sleeves or straps, you need a convertible bra. The best convertible bras are able to accommodate strapless, halter, and low-back styles with some brands even having crisscross or one shoulder options. To maximize flexibility, also look for a bra with a deep, plunging front, perfect for v-necks and scoop necks.

Panties

Seamless—When it comes to panties, the default style is seamless. No matter if you like briefs or boy shorts, thongs or bikinis, *seamless* is the way to go. Believe me, nothing disrupts your look like visible panty lines.

Hosiery

Sheer Pantyhose—An office staple, sheer pantyhose are as important now as they were 30 years ago.

Fishnet Tights—Ah, fishnets…how do I love thee? Let me count the ways. Always chic, always trendy, and always fashionable, fishnets are the best way to add a bit of spice to your regular, everyday wardrobe. The most important thing to remember with fishnets is the smaller the mesh, the better.

Opaque Black Tights–Who hasn't gone a winter without wearing black tights? Not only do they keep your legs warm, they're great for transitioning summer dresses into fall…not to mention making your legs look long and slender.

Garter Belt & Stockings–I put these two items together because you really can't have one without

the other. A garter belt and stockings is the classic splurge…one that will make you feel and look as sexy as you already *are*.

Shapewear

Shaping Slip–It smoothes, it firms, and it shapes giving you the picture perfect hourglass figure with no trouble at all. The best shapewear is both pretty and practical.

Sleepwear

Robe–We're rounding out the list with a robe. Yes. A robe is the sort of thing that every woman needs…be it to lounge around the house, carry with you on vacation, or run to the mailbox for the paper. A good robe is soft, simple, and flattering.

Acquire the 10 pieces of lingerie every woman needs in her underwear drawer and consider two more lingerie-related products I highly recommend you own keep to your lingerie in like-new condition…a good detergent and a sturdy, spacious lingerie wash bag. Both are available for next-to-nothing and they are more than worth the cost.

I would go as far as to say that the cost of not revamping your lingerie drawer is far more expensive than the investment.

"I love the confidence that makeup gives me."
Tyra Banks

47

DAY 9: WEAR MAKEUP
THE 5 MINUTE FACE

When you have been in a rut, the last thing you are thinking about is fixing up. You see others and you admire their looks but you can't seem to focus on anything but the situation you find yourself in. The good news is it is YOUR TIME! You are the key actress of your life's role. Your can now take center stage and not your situation.

So, let's talk about the 5-minute face. Because it need not take a lot of time to *look* like a million bucks!

Challenge time!

Concealer

Need to hide under-eye circles or a blemish that just popped up? It only takes about 30 seconds to apply concealer. You can use concealer before or after your foundation -- experts are split on which is best. Experiment and find out what works for you. Use a very small amount of concealer (you don't want the product to get cake-y) and pat it into your skin, rather than rubbing. You can use a brush, sponge or your fingertips. Pick a shade that is very close to your natural skin tone.

Eye liner or shadow

Pick one -- you don't need both when you are in a hurry. If you want a simple, natural look, just sweep eye shadow in a neutral tone over your lid. If you want your eyes to stand out, apply eye liner instead. Line just your upper lashes. Apply just one coat of mascara so you don't have to wait the time between coats. Doing your eyes shouldn't take more than a minute or two.

BB cream

BB cream is a multipurpose product that should be part of every busy woman's makeup routine. Popular in Asia for years, BB cream is now all the rage in America. This product can illuminate, hydrate, nourish and even out your skin. The coverage isn't heavy, but generally not as sheer as tinted moisturizer. With some BB creams, you can skip the foundation, concealer, highlighter, sunscreen, anti-aging serum and moisturizer. It can cover pimples, minimize the look of pores, hide fine lines and wrinkles, smooth your complexion and brighten your skin. BB cream can be worn on its own or in conjunction with mineral makeup.

Bronzer or blush

Get your glow on with a little bronzer or blush.

This is especially important if your natural complexion is a little pasty. Use a light hand -- you don't need much color to make a difference. When it comes to bronzer, make sure it's not more than a shade or two darker than your natural skin tone.

Lip gloss

Put the finishing touch on your face with a dab of lip gloss. It takes just a few seconds to apply lip gloss and you can do it while you are heading out the door. If you prefer lipstick, take the time to use liner, too. Before applying lipstick, line your lip then fill them in entirely with the pencil. This will give your lipstick a nice base and make it last much longer.

"To this day, I don't like people walking on stage not looking good. You have to look good. If you feel special about yourself then you're going to play special."
Benny Goodman

DAY 10: TAKE A DAY OF RESTORATION

After a few years your husband no longer
recognizes you! Where is his wife? You're in a
rut because life happens. Kids, careers,
laundry, cooking, cleaning, and more repeating.
Understandable. But now is your time! It is time
to get out of the rut you have been in by first
acknowledging you are in one and that you are
not taking the best care of yourself.

Think back to when you were dating your
husband... your boyfriend. You went all out.
Long showers, bath soaks in your favorite
bubbly, every hair was in place, you spent an
hour pondering over outfits and your
undergarments were on lock! Tell me I am off-
base and you can stop reading. But if I am on it,
read like your marriage depends on it.
Today you are charged with a long shower to
start your day and a long bath to end you day.
Move heaven and earth to make it happen.
Today is about restoration. I want you to
restore your old ritual of occasional, long baths
and extended showers, leaving you in a state
of relaxation. No rushing, no scurrying; sheer
indulgence. The very scent of you should ignite
energy within. Exfoliate with a scrub, lather and
shave for glistening skin. Add some scented oil
to your bath.
He misses you. The real you. The scent only
you carry. *The you* that is a sexy *beast*!

By exercising good personal hygiene, and showing that we care about ourselves, we are also showing that we care about them. Our spouse likes to see us looking our best. That's why they were attracted to us in the first place, and why they eventually married us. If we don't keep ourselves looking our best, we run the risk that they will not be as attracted to us as they once were, and this is not a good thing. It may not lead to cheating, but it will lead to a reduction in intimacy, and that's not good for a marriage. Your spouse may love you for who you are, but don't take that for granted.

Go the extra mile like you used to before *life got in the way.* Some of what Day 11 has in store for you will help you muster the energy.

"My grandmother started walking five miles a day when she was sixty. She's ninety-seven now, and we don't know where the heck she is."

Ellen DeGeneres

DAY 11: BEGIN A 30-MINUTE/DAY
BOOST SESSION

Can gaining muscle tone, stamina and strength help you project a better body image and increase your confidence? I thought so, too.

Today begins your *boost session*. Schedule out your boost sessions for 5 times a week, without fail, starting today.

For your *boost session*, opt for cardio (stationary bike, elliptical, walking/light jogging) for three days and resistance training (low weights, high reps) the other two days.

I chose to use the *boost session* instead of *workout* because many women stuck in *blah-dom* associate *workout* with pain. Rather, I want you to think of exercise as a boost to your day. It is giving back to yourself, a treat that you deserve. It need not be an a 2-hour ordeal. Getting your heart rate up for 30 minutes a day pays off in huge dividends. Here are a few of the fringe benefits of your boost session.

-Increases your metabolism
-Helps you sleep better
-Improves your sexual performance
-Improved mental acuity
-Strengthens your immune system
-Slows the aging process

-Reduces your risk of premature death
-Builds healthy muscles, bones and joints
-Increases your energy and endurance
_Restores your libido
_Improves your confidence
_Reduces stress, anxiety and depression
_Reduces the risk of many diseases

Just one of these listed benefits is enough to spring into action. The comprehensive list will have you wondering what took you so long!

On Day 12 it gets better!

"Good plans shape good decisions. That's why good planning helps elusive dreams come true."
Geoffrey Fisher

DAY 12: POST YOUR MEALS AHEAD

You know the saying, if you fail to plan, you plan to fail. Answer this. How has your nutrition been in the past few months? How has your weight been in the past few months? How many fast-food receipts are cluttering your pocketbook? Hmmm.

Today you will begin journaling everything you eat and drink and you will plan and post all meals in a software program prior to consumption. No midnight runs to McDonald's, lunch runs to Panera Bread or impulse runs to Starbucks unless they are *planned.* I know, Starbucks is a hard one. Indulge me.

There are several free downloadable apps, such as My Fitness Pal and Weight Watchers, for your Apple or Droid phone that will allow you to post, monitor and track your eating habits. Go ahead and register today.

Begin to become more aware of your routines as well. *When* you eat is just as important to balancing your diet as what you eat. Establish a schedule based on your lifestyle that makes sense. EX. Here's my typical daily eating schedule:

-I have breakfast at around 7 AM.
-I'll have a small snack at around 10 AM.
-Lunch is between noon and 1 PM.

-I'll have a small snack at around 3 PM.
-I eat my dinner around 7 PM.

Today's challenge is an imperative to your quest to reach *fierce*. By posting your meals you will eat healthier, shop more efficiently, save more money and enjoy a variety of foods. *Fierce* radiates from the inside out!

DAY 13: GIVE YOUR JEWELRY SOME TLC

In order to present the image you wish to convey and let you personality shine through there is no simpler way than with a jewelry wardrobe that creates a polished finish. Today, your challenge is to make note of what you have and don't have in this below list of eight, basic jewelry wardrobe staples and pick up at least one.

-Pearl Stud Earrings
-Diamond Solitaire Earrings
-Hoop Earrings
-Diamond Solitaire Pendant
-Pearl Strand or Pearl Station Necklace
-Gold Bracelet
-Gold Chain Necklace
-Signature Piece in your most flattering gemstone

Jewelopedia recommends we consider four things when expanding our jewelry wardrobe.

Consider size and scale. The taller you are, or bolder your personality, the more substantial or dramatic your pieces should be.

Next, *consider your budget*. Buy the best quality you can afford. Your metals should be gold, silver or platinum (gleaming silver is just as stunning as platinum at a fraction of the cost, but it does oxidize and needs to be cleaned regularly). Start out with freshwater pearls and move up to Akoya, Tahitianor South Sea pearls. If diamond solitaire earrings are not in the budget, buy CZ's or diamond clusters for now. Your signature piece can be as simple and inexpensive as a color-flattering gemstone pendant for your silver chain, or as intricate and pricey as a lacy woven gold bib necklace.

Consider your facial features. Do you have small, medium, or large features? This will determine the size of your pearls and diamonds. Diamond studs should be at least 1/4 ct each (4 mm) and pearls should be 6 mm or bigger.

Last, *consider your lifestyle.* A bangle bracelet is a timeless classic piece, but make sure it won't be in your way when you are working. You could also choose a gold chain bracelet, a cuff, or a gemstone bracelet. Perhaps you prefer your everyday hoops dressed up with a dangling pearl, or lined with diamonds if you can wear more sparkle for the things you do.

Your signature piece must be wearable for your lifestyle, so if you work with your hands all the time, your signature ring should have a low profile (pave or bezel set).

"CLUTTER IS POSTPHONED DECISIONS"
BARBARA HEMPHILL

DAY 14: PURGE & REPLACE

Your challenge today is to get organized and declutter. When we are disorganized it negatively impacts our finances, our relationships, our happiness, our health, our goals and our style! If it is taking you an hour to get dressed in the morning it may be because your closet is overflowing with items you cannot find, do not love and/or haven't worn in three years or more. Purge today.

Grab a few trash bags and clean out your closet. Bless someone if the clothes are in good condition. But do not hold onto items you know you do not wear in hopes of "one day". Bye-bye.

Next, clean out your makeup bag. Lipsticks, mascaras and foundations that have expired should be tossed and replaced. Clean your brushes and stow your cosmetics and toiletries nicely. Getting dressed should be something you look forward to. Having everything in its place and presentational will serve to enhance your experience.
Hang your clothes on nice velvet or wooden hangers and color-code the arrangement of your hanging garments for added ease in the mornings.

Snap a photo of your go-to outfits so that they

are heavily entrenched in your mind. Today will require some real work, but you deserve a fierce closet, a little piece of heaven. As the adage goes, to declutter your space is to declutter your mind.

Now that you have decluttered your environment, it is time to shop! The fun part! What did you get rid of?

_____
_____
_____
_____
_____
_____
_____
_____
_____
_____

What needs replacing? What do you need?

_____
_____
_____
_____
_____
_____
_____
_____
_____
_____

When you go shopping, resist the urge to judge while keeping in mind what you need to flesh out your wardrobe. Consider your personality, body type and lifestyle. Don't judge anything until you try it on and see if it looks good on you. Many things look a lot better than you may think from only seeing them hanging on the rack or folded up on a table. Here are some things you may notice. Catch yourself.

- Your self-image or a sense of discomfort with change may pop up here and make you think things like, "That's not me, I'm not the type of person who wears "this stuff" in response to styles that would look good on you. Try to ignore these thoughts and push out of your comfort zone. You may be surprised at how within a few days you're totally comfortable in outfits you initially dismissed as "not me".

- You may have some emotional baggage around certain styles, even though you think deep down that they look good. If you don't like the people who wear certain styles (e.g., red bottoms, hair extensions, expensive handbags) the idea of dressing like one of 'them' may seem traitorous to you.

Week Three:
Own It
(Do the Work)

DAY 15: LET YOUR HAIR DOWN

"When you allow yourself to wallow in frustration, you're continuing to wage war between prediction and observation. And wars of this nature have a tendency to self-perpetuate. This means that you'll continue to find new sources of conflict even as old ones dry up. As long as you believe that it's okay for prediction and observation to fight, your mind will continue to feed the battle with fresh troops, ammo, and supplies."

This is a powerful statement.

Throw caution to the wind today. Allow yourself the freedom to be free from frustration. It is all in your mind. When you realize that this conflict is pointless, which indeed it is, then you can consciously end it.

When I read this article by personal development guru Steve Pavlina (September 2012), I gasped because it made so much sense and answered a lot of questions I had the first time I opened my business and things were not happening as I predicted at first. I was feeling salty and frustrated.

Pavlina states that, "If you want to invite more abundance and flow into your life, you'll likely get much faster results not by pounding away on your desires but by releasing your resistance to what's already showing up — as well as any worries or concerns about what might happen next."

And who knew this? Keep reading.

"It's easier to start a business if you don't worry about going broke. It's easier to invite loving relationships if you don't worry about potential rejection. It's easier to write interesting articles if you don't worry about criticism.

I'm very happy with my life right now. This has been an amazingly beautiful year, and I'm excited about what's coming up in the next month or two. I'm looking forward to cool creative projects, lucrative business deals, warm and loving cuddle sessions, exciting travel adventures, yummy sex, new friends, new growth lessons, and more.

But I've learned that it's usually disastrous to let my predictions get too far ahead of my observations. I allow myself to enjoy the vibe of being already aligned with my desires, but I don't let myself get clingy with it.

If I become attached to certain predictions, then what happens if and when my observations fall short of my predictions? What happens if an expected business deal falls through, or a cuddle partner cancels, or a beautiful trip gets postponed? If I get clingy with my expectations, I'm inviting frustration.

I allow myself to make predictions — I can't really help that — but I let them float around continuously without declaring a solid lock. Only observation has the privilege and the responsibility of declaring a lock (and even then, that sometimes needs to be tamed as well). Prediction never gets to wield the baton of certainty. Prediction can only suggest, never assert. Prediction can only declare what may be, never what will be.

By releasing my attachment to what might be, and simply resting with my intentions, I avoid a great deal of frustration. Sure I screw up from time to time. But when I come to my senses, I tell prediction to surrender. I put him back in his proper position and remind him that he's a scout, not a general.

This requires patient practice."

So, what I learned was that part of being *fierce* is throwing caution to the wind, letting your hair down and not allowing frustration to quench your zeal, your tenacity and your creativity. What are some areas where you are anxious, frustrated and a worry wart?

_____

_____

_____

_____
_____
_____
_____
_____
_____
_____
_____
_____
_____
_____
_____
_____
_____
_____
_____
_____
_____
_____
_____
_____
_____

Your challenge today is to *release* them! Your practice starts today.

"Dress shabbily and they remember the dress; dress impeccably and they remember the woman."
Coco Chanel

DAY 16: EARMARK YOUR ASSETS

Every woman has something that she really likes about herself physically. Today I challenge you to get clear about and be able to articulate what your assets are in such a way that it rolls off of your tongue. Stand in the mirror and tell yourself what you love about yourself. I love the bridge of my nose. I like that I am curvy at a size 4 and curvy at a size 14. I like my smile.

Now taking those assets into consideration, intentionally earmark how you are going to play up those assets today. Will you wear color on your lips? Will you wear a sleeveless blouse? Will you wear heels? Will your toes be polished a new hue? Will your hair be up and off of your neck? Jot down your assets and your plans to play them up today.

_____
_____
_____
_____
_____
_____
_____
_____

**"The best colour in the whole world is the
one that looks good on you."
Coco Chanel**

DAY 17: KNOW YOUR GO-TO OUTFITS

Have you ever watched a relay race in track and field? Notice how the runner is already running when the baton is passed? Something tells me the runner already knows the baton is coming. Duh. Of course, it is! So, the runner has to be in position when the time comes to receive the baton.
Now that you have taken inventory of your wardrobe and earmarked your assets, it is time to plan your "go-to" outfits.

Identify your go-to outfits so that you are ready. Ready for whatever! Is it not frustrating to learn of a last minute *opportunity of a lifetime* where urgency is key and you are not prepared? Doesn't it just make you want to pull your hair out and scream? So that you make it to your engagement on time (sans sweating because you were rushing), show up ready, poised and in control.

Some suggestions for go-to outfits would be colors that make you feel fabulous, special items-- be it a pink lipstick, a mauve scarf or a red-bottom shoe), a crisp white, wrinkle-free blouse, a pencil skirt, dark denim and an LBD-- in shapes that suit your proportions and body type.

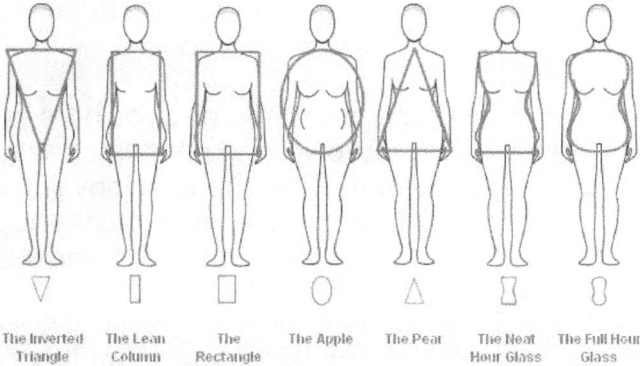

The Inverted Triangle   The Lean Column   The Rectangle   The Apple   The Pear   The Neat Hour Glass   The Full Hour Glass

I will quickly quench the notion that one body type is better than another. I often in my industry hear this and it makes me cringe. It is like saying apples are better than bananas. Count your blessings and not your blemishes. Bridgette Raes, author of Style Rx, says you have to dress for the body you have to create the body you want.

If you more of an apple figure, you tend to gain weight around the middle (or you simply want to hide a few post-pregnancy pounds), clothes should fit loosely around the midsection (to conceal a full stomach) and more snugly elsewhere (to play up thin limbs).

If you are more of a straight-up-and-down figure (often considered boyish, opt for styles that fit snugly at your middle but flare out at the bottom (whether it's a skirt or pants) to create curves. Avoid dresses that are tight all over and anything too flow-y or unstructured around the waist, like empire-waist tops.

The pear shape is defined as shoulders and torso that are narrower than the hips. Avoid shapeless, oversize sweaters; skinny jeans and pants; and skirts in a flimsy, curve-hugging fabric, like silk. Opt for A-line skirts and wide-leg pants.

You have an hourglass shape if you have an ample chest, a narrow waist, and full (but not wide) hips, this shape, although evenly proportioned, can seem as if it's all angles.

Avoid shapeless or boxy styles, like baby-doll dresses, tunics, and oversize cardigans. You should opt for staples such as high-waist pants and wrap shirts.

Also know that colors do matter. The right choice of colors can make a big difference between a look that works and one that doesn't. First, make sure that your body structure or skin type can carry off the right colors.

Pale complexions, for instance, might look washed out with neutral-colored apparel like light peach or champagne. On the other hand, black or ruby might bring out the delicacy of your porcelain complexion or bring color to your appearance. Then again, also make it a point to use the right colors to highlight your best features. For instance use solid and dark colors if you are on the heavier side, since these absorb light and give the illusion of being slender. Learn more about color charting which lets you wear every single color there is but by making sure that you wear the right shade and tone of every color.

Today, whatever your body type may be, check for items that fit your proportions and make you look and feel fabulous! Jot them down.

_____

_____

_____

_____

_____

_____

_____

_____

_____

_____

_____

_____

_____

_____

"A woman who doesn't wear perfume has no future."
Coco Chanel

DAY 18: PICK OUT A NEW SCENT THAT REMINDS YOU OF YOUR POWER

That's right, pick out a new scent today and spritz in on. Ahhhhh... Now, isn't that nice?

I recently read an article in Harper's Bazaar (Gaitskill) entitled, *The Power of Perfume*. It was quite intriguing. The opening paragraph said it all.

"The appeal of perfume is that it is at once ephemeral and empowering. It creates a shimmering invisible armor that lingers in a room long after its wearer has gone and infuses our imagination with a subtle power, hinting at a hidden identity." The isolated scent alone of a perfume can take you to an era, a place, a memory, a state of mind. That is indeed powerful.

In Woman's Day (Gottesman) there was a study reported on the power of scent, reporting that once you associate a particular scent with a certain emotion, just smelling it in the future may conjure up the same emotions.

To find out which scents are most likely to have the greatest impact they investigated the latest studies on aromatherapy and aromocology (A.K.A. the study of scent and its effect on

mental and physical health).
Did you know that just smelling roses or
sniffing coffee in the morning will perk you up
all day?
Wow!

If the smell of *rose* does it, imagine what
perfume does. Fragrances can boost your
mood, boost your confidence and increase
your attraction.

The aromatherapy benefits of perfume make it
worth its weight in gold. Some of the benefits
include boosted energy, stress-relief and
productivity.

Amazingly, when you smell good, you feel
good and you have the confidence to perform
even when hesitation sets in. Men and women
are attracted to what they see, the energy a
person radiates and the way a person smells. It
is much like a signature.

Just remember that no two people smell the
same wearing the same perfume. So choose
wisely! You will fall in love with the scent and
you will know it when you smell it!

Tomorrow you will be so glad you bought this.

"I wanted to give a woman comfortable clothes that would flow with her body. A woman is closest to being naked when she is well-dressed."
Coco Chanel

DAY 19: WEAR YOUR BEST LINGERIE UNDERNEATH IT ALL

Once you have the basics down it is time to have a little fun with your lingerie. This is not about him, this is about *you.* He just gets to enjoy *whatever is going on with you* as well.

By now you should have already ditched the granny panties. You know the matching bras and panties you've been saving for someone special? When you wear them they will likely make you feel pretty, even confident. Instead of waiting to show them off, give yourself the pleasure of putting them on no matter what the occasion.

Of course, your significant other will no doubt appreciate it if you spice up your undergarments, but the important thing is that your wearing something beautiful under your clothes will make *you* feel fabulous and in charge.

Because nothing stifles sexy like lacking confidence, always make sure that whatever you wear over your lingerie, follows the same tailored shape as your undergarments. You want nothing to be out of the ordinary. Again, this is for you, not others.

So, strut your stuff, knowing you have it going on even down to the skinny. Your added confidence will certainly not go unnoticed and your energy level may even get you into doors once closed. One thing is for sure—you will feel empowered.

DAY 20: VISIT THE SHOE PARLOR & TAILOR

From hair and skin to clothes and shoes, one's appearance is a constant trigger of snap judgments. Whether interviewing for a job or just looking to make a good first impression, a recent perception study conducted by Kelton for Invisalign, proves that even the alignment of teeth is a catalyst for assumptions regarding success, popularity, intelligence, and general health.

The most common rebuttal I get from clients who come to me for change is "that's not me". Keep in mind, being them has not been working for them but I push them to not make snappy judgments but to let it marinate a few days. After a few days of noticeable attitude shifts from co-workers, extra whistles at the grocery store and more self-assurance, they are on cloud nine with the same duds they were quick to dismiss Day 1.

Resistance to change is normal. But, in being fierce you cannot allow it to stop you from improving yourself.

Your favorite go-to suit in your closet is too baggy in the inseam and your look is suffering, appearing sloppy and inexpensive at best. A quick run to the tailor can have you looking like a million bucks. When clothing fits and is tailor-made to fit your contours, you instinctively project, and others instinctively perceive, a richer experience with you. You command an elevated presence than the woman wearing the off-the rack suit with the hanging inseam.

The same is true of your shoes. Your favorite stilettos should be treated with tender loving care. Otherwise, are they really your favorite stilettos? I would hate to see your lease favorite. Smile.
Take a quick look at your shoe wardrobe. Pull out shoes you want to keep but that need some care due to wear. You can make them new again with a run to the shoe parlor.

Have your favorite "it" shoes and ill-fitting clothes tailored to a tee. Today. I challenge you!

DAY 21: WORK YOUR FACE SHAPE

Today's challenge requires identifying your face shape and donning a complimenting hairstyle that you love Share this with your hairstylist. If getting a cut, make sure the service is being provided by a master stylist versed in cuts. Many women do not know their face shape let alone know that certain hairstyles complement certain face shapes better than others.

Here are a few examples:

Round faces look good with piece-y bobs, sleek ponytails, uneven bobs, defined pixies, long layers, angled bobs, asymmetrical cuts and uneven cuts (hair is not all the same length).

Oval faces look good with bobs with side bangs, center parts, blunt bangs, and edgy short cuts.

Square faces look good with tousled shags, thinned out bobs, wavy ends, and long & straight hair.

Heart-shaped faces look good with bouncy bobs, deep side parts, long, layered waves, and pixies with side-swept bangs.

Spotted *FIERCE*

The right style and the right cut can seriously raise your style IQ.

Week Four: Flaunt It (Blah who?)

"It's the fire in my eyes,
And the flash of my teeth,
The swing in my waist,
And the joy in my feet.
I'm a woman
Phenomenally."
Maya Angelou

DAY 22: DRESS UP FOR NO REASON

You will never—I repeat—*never*, improve your sense of style if your default look is "I give up". Unacceptable.

Nothing beats the rush you feel when you see your reflection in a window and love what you see. Today the quest on the table is to dress up for absolutely no reason other than it is what you do. You are re-writing the rules, recalibrating your expectations of yourself. Even if you live in a city where no one has style, you be the change you want to see. You be the jet-setter. You set the standard. Let your environment conform to you; not the other way around.

Forbes posted an interesting article called *Are You Dressing the Part of Your Job? (ForbesWoman, April 2011)* on dressing the part. I pulled out a few of my favorite quotes, sure to resonate with you.

"The right clothes also help the actor get into character, affecting posture and attitude. Turn the sound off of your TV and you'll still know what the characters do for a living. And where they land on the food chain."

"It's about trust and credibility. The reptilian part

SHEKINA FARR MOORE

of our brain tells us to trust what we see more than any other sense. And trust what the person is wearing."

"Several well-known studies from the 1960s involving lab coats, prison guard uniforms and electric shocks show we are more likely to rely on uniforms as an indicator of expertise and authority, than not. Robert Cialdini, a New York Times bestselling classic, Influence, also has some interesting things to say about uniforms listed under one of his Six Weapons of Influence."

While reading a blog post on Why You Should Dress To Impress---The ROI of Fashion, I was very impressed with the authors (two young men) and their ability to eloquently articulate the ways perceived success translates. These bloggers take you through a continuum of their "bum years", "their breakthrough", and their "boss years".

Through progressive improvements in dress they were able to command more money for their services (the same services offered in their "bum years") due to perceived credibility. During their *bum years* their hourly consulting rate was below $100.

Equipped with new clothes, a new haircut and new shoes, when it came down to locking in new deals these potential customers started offering more money. Their hourly consulting rate at this point was at $250. As they got a taste of money making, they wanted more, so they decided to take things up a new level with their wardrobe. This was the boss level that changed the game.

Here is one blogger's enlightening testimony about his *boss years:*

"From Gucci suits, to designer shoes, to 5 figure watches, I stepped up my appearance as much as I could within my financial constraints. And boy, not only was there a huge ROI, but it was a much bigger difference than I ever experienced between my bum and normal stage.

By dressing to impress, successful business owners started to flock to me when I attended networking events and people listened when I spoke in business meetings. In addition to that I was praised for wearing rare watches that other business owners wanted, but didn't have.

This experience taught me that successful people like to hang around with other successful people as they tend to feel comfortable around themselves. Now, by no means am I saying that all successful people dress nice, but the chances are if someone comes up to you and they are wearing a 5 figure watch, they have money.

And when you start talking about business with

93

these successful people, they know that if they do business with you, it's going to be costly for the following reasons:

- ***You have an expensive lifestyle*** *– if people realize you have money, they know that they are going to have to pay a pretty penny to work with you. They know that if you throw around small amounts of cash in front of you, you just won't care.*

- ***It has to move your needle*** *– in business there is saying that if it doesn't move your needle, it's not worth doing. So if the amount someone is willing to offer you isn't life changing, there is a much greater chance that you won't accept it. Due to this business owners will throw out much larger amounts if they want to work with you.*

By dressing like a "boss" my credibility went through the roof with other business owners and I was able to do things like close 7 figure business deals."

During the *boss years* their hourly consulting rate was above 4 figures. This is a vividly inspiring account of how much dress plays an important role in our perceived worth in the marketplace. How moving from *blah to fierce* can really pay off!

I especially love this blogger's commentary as

it speaks to establishing your worth:

"I'm sure most of the people reading this blog are familiar with the Zukerberg "hoodie". Once you have wealth (Neil's article on wealth is pretty good), not to be confused with riches, you can pretty much wear whatever you want. Some of the wealthiest people I know are perfectly comfortable in cargo shorts and a regular shirt. One of the multi-millionaires I know was a guy who was working for minimum wage at the same store I was working at as a teenager.

When I found out about his real financial situation I was more than surprised. However, that was simply his choice because he didn't want to be at home all day and loved to interact with people. And I was only doing what we all, as humans, naturally do. We judge. Taking that into consideration, when I was first starting to meet the rich and powerful and getting them to give me their money, I was extremely nervous and out of my realm. I was almost afraid to ask for money. But the amount you say you're worth establishes credibility. If a guy came up to you and said, "Dude I'll sell you my brand new Bentley for $1,000," you would be wondering what was wrong with it. So I started buying some power suites and utilizing patterns that emphasized my 6'5" stature.

I found out that if you are tall and can make

yourself look powerful, people have this subconscious and psychological behavior to want to impress you or make you happy. If you pay attention to social environments, you can really learn a lot for your advantage."

Here is the question of the day.

How much ROI are you leaving on the table by not dressing to impress? Your challenge today and every day is to dress to impress. Not enough can be said for impeccable dress that commands a room.

"Walk amongst the natives by day, but in your heart be Super[wo]man."
Gene Simmons

DAY 23: SMILE LIKE YOU ARE KEEPING THE STEAMIEST SECRET

A new day! So much to be thankful for! Look around! Smiling yet? Today's challenge is simple. Smile. Conjure up the steamiest of secrets and snicker about it all day today.

The rewards of smiling are countless but they boil down to making you feel happier. You mean to tell me all I have to do is smile and it can make me feel better? Yes. That is what I am saying.

Here are some other advantages *smilers* experience:

--looking younger
--a better mood
--lower blood pressure
--released endorphins
--stress relief
--improved immune system

Mark Stibich, PhD., says, "Smiling is a great way to make yourself stand out while helping your body to function better. Smile to improve your health, your stress level, and your attractiveness."

For those of you who don't like your smile, do something about it. Like you, I used to not like my smile. People told me it was great but I

didn't like my overbite. Right before my
wedding I decided to get braces. I did. Many
tried to reason with me that it was a bad time to
consider braces but I knew what was best for
me. I wanted to go into my marriage having
made that decision for myself to improve
myself. I did and it was the best decision I ever
made. I have never regretted the decision to
act now and follow my own gut. The short
inconvenience was well-worth the decades of
a glowing smile I have enjoyed. My confidence
went to another level, my smile projects
confidence and my image projects success.

The lesson is, let nothing and no one get in the
way of or rob you of your smile. It is a reflection
of your soul.

Smile!

DAY 24: GO OUT ON *GIRLS' NIGHT OUT* LOOKING HOT AS EVER

Tonight's challenge is going to be so much fun! Enough with the work already, right? Well, here is the kicker. Not only is incorporating tonight's challenge into your lifestyle ongoing going to benefit you it is going to benefit your significant other.

When you go out looking hot as ever, other men will flirt with you. How does this benefit your significant other, you ask? Well, as a woman it will make you feel sexy and desirable. While this might initially sound unacceptable to you, remember that you don't actually want to go home with a man you flirt with in a bar or a club or at dinner with the girls. But it does feel good to take it out on your love.

When you return home your sexual appetite will be revved up, and your husband will reap the benefits of other men's labor. How about that? Stop the negative thinking if you are going to be *fierce*, you must own your power.

Scheduling girls' night out and consistently making it apart of your lifestyle will also help you remember what it is like to be single and appreciate your courtship!

Your man obviously trusts you which signifies an underlying stability in your relationship which has to be both comforting and exciting.

By going out you are also providing outlet time for your beau. He, too, will be experiencing freedom and appreciate coming home to *you. Oh, la-la!*

Instead of venting and laying all the gossip on your significant other because you have no outlet, you have a system in place that allows you to do what you *need* to do and be heard. Men are problem-solvers, not the best listeners. So, save yourself the drama of getting mad when he doesn't listen to your venting and share with girls who get it. And look hot while you do it.

There. Now, let's talk about looking hot. Looking hot is not putting it all out there. It is about earmarking your assets as discussed in Day 16. Whatever your asset is, highlight it. If it is your legs and they will be fanning in the wind tonight, do not also have your upper body fanning in the wind.

Pick one area to highlight. For this reason when I decide to highlight my lips I do not highlight my eyes. Doing so, defeats the purpose and causes confusing competition for attention. It also looks like you are trying too hard. Simplicity is elegant. A three-quarter sleeve dress with a with high neckline but high hem-line will do the trick for the woman with fabulous gams.

Alternatively, skinny jeans, heels a tank and chunky necklace with coordinating bangle can have just as much appeal.

Gauge your looks by fit, proportions and how they make you feel! The way you feel will radiate and will certainly have your girlfriends wondering what is going on with you... But don't tell...Shhhhh...

"Sex appeal is fifty percent what you've got and fifty percent what people think you've got."
Sophia Loren

DAY 25: INTENTIONALLY WALK WITH AN ADDED PEP IN YOUR STEP

Pep is described as high spirits, high energy and vitality. It is an intangible quality that is altogether irresistibly appealing. Your challenge today is to walk with a pep in your step, a glow, and to keep it radiating. How?

Be kind

Say thank-you often, offer compliments, tell your co-workers and employees how much you appreciate them. Take a few minutes to do that each day and watch what happens.

Identify your style for added ownership

Hire an image consultant. It is extremely important to keep in mind that dressing right has little to do with fashion and everything to do with style. This is because style relates directly to your individual dressing sense which in turn depends on your personal physical features. Hence you may not have a size-zero figure or be able to afford the most expensive labels and yet have an impressive sense of style or dressing sense.

Now, if you want a style that is all your own, you need to tailor it according to your own physical dimensions and not copy what the models on the ramp are wearing. So go for an honest evaluation of your body type-- whether you are thin, fat, tall and short. Pay attention to certain aspects of your body, like an ample behind or a short neck.

Once you have made a careful mental note of your physical characteristics, it will be easy for you to evolve the right style by highlighting your plus points and minimizing your negative features. For instance if you happen to have a petite figure, go for vertical stripes as they give an impression of length and avoid horizontal stripes which will make you look even shorter. An image consultant can assist you with your style identity and a course of action that works for your lifestyle, shape and personality.

Follow a healthy lifestyle

Finally an attractive personal style doesn't end with buying the right clothes and expensive accessories. You need glowing skin, healthy hair and a fit body to look great on the whole. So don't minimize the importance of following a healthy lifestyle which includes a nutritious well-balanced diet, around thirty minutes of exercise every day as well as avoiding harmful habits like smoking.

Load up on anti-oxidant rich fresh fruits and vegetables in and between your meals and stay away from fried foods as well as refined, processed products. Regular exercise will not only keep your system healthy but also your tone up your figure which in turn will allow you to dress well and attract the guy you want to.

DAY 26: GET A MENTOR

All *fierce* women have mentors. Unlike *blah* women we are not so casual about our futures. We are passionate and understand that having a mentor only sharpens *and strengthens* the saw. Mentees gain invaluable insight beyond their own education and experience. Give yourself the edge with the support and guidance of a mentor.

Whether you need advice or a sounding board, a mentor can inspire and guide you. Your benefits may extend far beyond what you planned, and may include:
- Access to a support system during critical stages of your academic and/or career development
- An insider's perspective on navigating your career/industry pathway
- Clearer understanding and enhancement of academic and career plans
- Exposure to diverse perspectives and experiences
- Direct access to powerful resources within your profession
- Identification of skill gaps
- Greater knowledge of career success factors

- The foundation of a lasting professional network

107

Mentors benefit as well by building their own leadership skills, helping other succeed, supporting the industry and profession and leaving a legacy. So, if you are afraid to seek out a mentor consider what *Fierce Amy* would do and consider that mentors benefit in the following ways:

- Exposure to the emerging talent pool
- Ongoing attention to their own career development
- The satisfaction of imparting wisdom and experience to others without a huge time commitment
- Enhancement of coaching, leadership, management, and recruiting skills
- Exposure to diverse thoughts, styles, personalities, and cultures
- Opportunities for recruitment to their profession and/or employment setting
- A way to give back to their association and/or profession

- A lasting career network

Fierce Amy would be all over this. What would *Fierce* _____ (plug in your name) do?

This is your challenge today. Contact three (3) mentors.

1. _____
2. _____
3. _____

Above, jot down the names of (3) mentors you could learn from. Aim high. Think of (3) mentors who possess the qualities listed below.

-Caring
-Open and honest
-Available
-Focused
-Similar Goals
-Positive
-Believe in You
-Open-minded
-Experienced
-Character

Consider looking for a mentor that is outside of your immediate environment and when you reach out to the mentor be clear in your expectations of the relationship.
Here are some guidelines taken from Modern Ms. Darcy when meeting with your potential mentor:

1. Be polite. Remember: you're asking for a favor! And you'll likely be nervous about asking, and it's easy to be less-than-socially-graceful when you're nervous. Being aware of this can help you make sure you sound friendly and not aloof. (This is an easy mistake to make—ask me how I know!)

2. Tell them why. *Your prospective mentor wants to know why you're asking them and not somebody else. Tell them why. Tell them what you think they have to offer; tell them why they're a good fit. You're much more likely to get a "yes" if you give them a good reason.*

3. Be specific. *What are you looking for? Don't just ask them, "Will you mentor me?" Be very specific about what you need help with, what form you want help to come in, and what you envision your meetings looking like. Make a specific request so they know what they're agreeing to. You're much more likely to get a "yes" if you're specific.*

4. Make it easy for them. *Be clear that you will suit their schedule. Do they want to skype or phone chat? Say yes. Do they want to meet at the coffee shop right by their office? Say yes. Do they want to meet at 6:00 am, or 9:00 pm. Say yes. Make it easy for them.*

Money Makin' Mom Columnist Deanna Hamilton wrote a book on mentorship that delves deeper into the incredible role mentorship plays in the lives of great women. It is called *The Great Mentor*. I highly recommend this book to gain clarity on the deeper, underlying meaning of the mantle.

Take this challenge seriously. You will be so glad you picked up the heavy phone and made contact with the leaders you jotted down! On the road to being *fierce* you sure make me proud! Your confidence is so becoming.

"Confidence is going after Moby Dick in a rowboat and taking the tartar sauce with you."
Zig Ziglar

DAY 27: BLOW HIS MIND

Today's challenge is to blow his mind! Get back to *date mode* where you pull out all the stops.

-Be capable of carrying on a conversation!
-Make sure your hair is soft!
-Let your personality shine through!
-Be stylish!
-Be open!
-Beam!
-Be Adventurous!
-Every once in a while, spontaneously skip out on work and every other responsibility in the world and just enjoy each other.

Lisa Pankau shares that intimacy through vulnerability is powerful advising the following to connect with your partner.

---

5 Ways to experience intellectual intimacy

---

1. Have a meaningful conversation about something that emotes and moves your partner's soul. Then ask your partner to share one of *your* topics of passion.
2. Together, discuss your most inspirational moments and the reasons they were so moving.
3. Share your life aspirations, and make a plan to help each other attain those

goals and dreams (no matter how unrealistic they seem -- because what the mind believes, it can achieve).

4. Have a meal together (with no television or other distractions), and take the time to hear what is going on in your partner's life. Then share the same with him.

5. Have a conversation about something you do not necessarily agree on, and then agree to disagree. This should increase awareness and understanding for the reasoning behind the belief systems that you each hold.

Imagine looking great, not having shared the 30 Day Challenge with your partner, to have him wondering all this time what has gotten into you and then to have such an intimate conversation that reconnects you on a spiritual and intellectual level.
It sounds like a set up to rock his world!

Pankau goes on to share that social intimacy is greatly intertwined with the other aspects of intimacy.

If you take the time to share experiences together, you can grow in *other* areas of intimacy. You never know what life experiences can bring to you personally or as a couple.

114

5 Ways to experience social intimacy

1. Have a date night one night per week.
2. Go for a walk on the beach, watch a sunset or experience some quiet time together.
3. Participate in some activity outside of your normal routine to build "together experiences" and memories.
4. Do something you would not normally do that your partner enjoys, and ask the same of him.

5. Remember that just because you are married or that you are involved in a long-term relationship, courtship never ends! Treat every day as if you were in the beginning stages of your relationship, and enjoy the newness that every day brings.

Relationships can be complicated in this society of hustle and bustle but, *fierce* women make it happen. You have the goods. Use the tools!

The reconnecting with your partner will not only blow his mind, it will blow yours!

DAY 28: PASS THE BATON

Today culminates a full four weeks that you have been working on you. You have been working to get yourself out of a rut and on with your destiny. All you needed was a little nudge. Some days were more challenging than others, but now your mind cannot go backward because it has already expanded. Once it is has experienced and is used to *fierce*, it cannot, will not, go back to *blah*.

Your challenge today is to harness the power you have experienced in gaining control over your situation and to pay it forward to another woman. Jot down a few names of women you know that come to mind; women you know who are in a rut. It is nothing they have said, it is written all over their faces. They think they are hiding but, like you once were, they are sending signals loud and clear that they need rescue.

Write down their names here.

1.
_____
2.
_____
3.
_____

Now, call each of these women right now and tell her that you would like to meet briefly with her in 3 days (Why? This is *after* you have *completed* your journey). Tell her you have something to share with her that will change her life!

SHEKINA FARR MOORE

Week Five:
Reflect It

118

**"Believe in yourself and there will come a
day when others will have no choice but to
believe with you."
Cynthia Kersey**

DAY 29: WRITE DOWN THE CHANGES YOU HAVE NOTICED ABOUT YOURSELF

We are almost finished with our time together. I would like for you to know that I am so very proud of you. Your courage recognized you were stuck in *blah-dom* and taking this journey was no light feat.

Today's challenge is for you to take an introspective look at the past 29 days. Write down any physical, emotional, psychological, spiritual changes you have noticed about yourself.

_____
_____
_____
_____
_____
_____
_____
_____
_____
_____
_____
_____
_____
_____

DAY 30: WRITE DOWN THE CHANGES YOU HAVE NOTICED IN OTHERS' INTERACTIONS WITH YOU

Take a few moments to reflect on the past 30 days. Reflect on all of your interactions with strangers, colleagues, your husband, your boyfriend, co-workers, family, church members, associations and friends.

What have you noticed?

_____
_____
_____
_____
_____
_____
_____
_____
_____
_____
_____
_____
_____
_____
_____
_____
_____
_____
_____
_____
_____
_____

**Congratulations!
You are
CERTIFIED FIERCE!!!**

Follow our movement on social media

Facebook
@BlahtoFierce

Hashtags

#blahtofierce
#thatfiercelife
#girlbefierce

Visit online

www.girlbefierce.com

"Don't be surprised by your greatness. Be surprised that no one expected it."
Rebecca Maizel, *Infinite Days*

ABOUT THE FIERCE GIRL EMPOWERMENT MOVEMENT

An unapologetic stance women and girls are taking as they posture themselves to impact their communities and beyond. Once a girl embraces her worth there is nothing she cannot do.
Our Fierce events and programs empower girls with healthy body image, esteem, and leadership tools needed in a global marketplace.

FIERCE GIRL EMPOWERMENT MOVEMENT

ABOUT THE AUTHOR
SHEKINA FARR MOORE

Shekina Moore, Ed.S., Pegged a Girls Advocate, Shekina Moore, Ed.S., is the visionary behind the Fierce Girl Empowerment Movement ™ (F.I.E.R.C.E. G.E.M.).

She believes helping to develop healthy esteem and positive body image in girls is the key to tapping into their leadership capacity. She holds three degrees and worked extensively in the school systems of North Carolina. All the years working with youth, Shekina began to notice that girls really did not have a voice. Too often, as she experienced, we fail to recognize girls for their invaluable contributions, placing too much emphasis on their physicality. One day Shekina was watching a documentary on girls that sparked something in her.

Where are the voices? Who is standing up for our girls?

Answering that call, her movement includes the Tween Star Awards™ (a platform that is showcasing and celebrating tween and teen girls who are shining in their communities), the Fierce Challenge ™, Tween Style Power ™,

128

G.E.M.'s Annual AuthenticiTea & Social and Blah to F.I.E.R.C.E.™ The Live Event.

A seven-time personal development Author, Shekina was named one of 52 Empowering Women Who Empower Girls along with The One World Doll Project's Stacey McBride-Irby, HGTV Property Virgin's Egypt Sherrod and WNBA President Laurel Richie. Featured in a host of publications, radio and TV shows, Shekina was also selected as a national semi-finalist for Proctor & Gamble's My Black Is Beautiful Ambassador Search (2014) and is listed among the Who's Who in Black Atlanta.

A wife, mom, mentor and big sister to many girls Shekina likes to bake, read and spend quality time with her family.

For more on the author visit:

www.girlbefierce.com

JOIN ME AND HELP ME RECOGNIZE GIRLS AGES 10-17 FOR THEIR VALUABLE CONTRIBUTIONS TO SOCIETY.

"I remember like yesterday the day fierce walked in the room of my heart. I began to eat, sleep, breathe, exude fierce. It was the day I decided to stop playing small and to take control of my life. People began to ask me what I was doing differently, to compliment me on my aura, to take notice when I entered the landscape.

Awareness, action, intensity and consistency had finally started to show up in my life and there was nothing I could do to stop it from being evident. When you're fierce, everyone knows it, and once you catch this fierce, there is no turning back. I look forward to hearing about the day fierce walked into your room. Much success to you."

-Shekina

Shekina Moore
GIRLS ADVOCATE

WHAT'S NEXT?

BLAH TO FIERCE FOR TEACHERS

BLAH TO FIERCE FOR TEEN GIRLS

BLAH TO FIERCE FOR FIRST LADIES

BLAH TO FIERCE: LADY SOLDIER TO LADY CIVILIAN

www.ingramcontent.com/pod-product-compliance
Lightning Source LLC
Chambersburg PA
CBHW072155090426
42740CB00012B/2278